easy GUITAR play along

ROCK SONGS FOR BEGINNERS

ISBN 978-1-4768-1762-0

HAL•LEONARD®
CORPORATION

7777 W. BLUEMOUND RD. P.O. BOX 13819 MILWAUKEE, WI 53213

Visit Hal Leonard Online at
www.halleonard.com

Are You Gonna Be My Girl

Words and Music by Cameron Muncey and Nicholas Cester

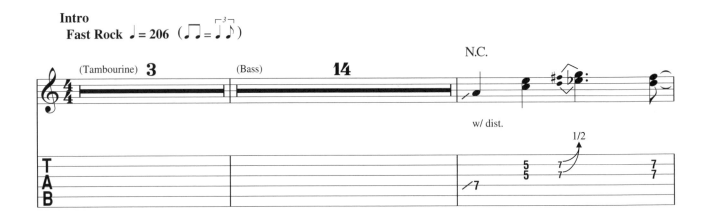

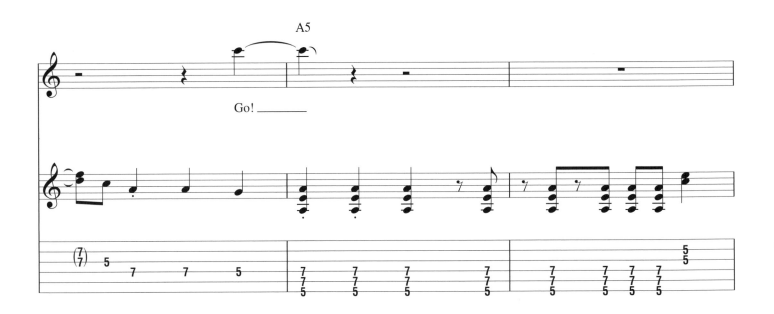

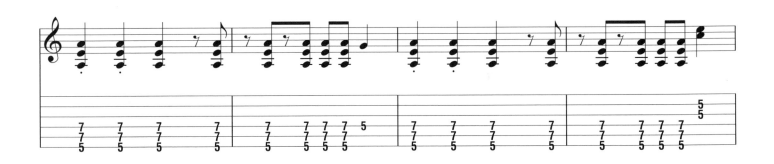

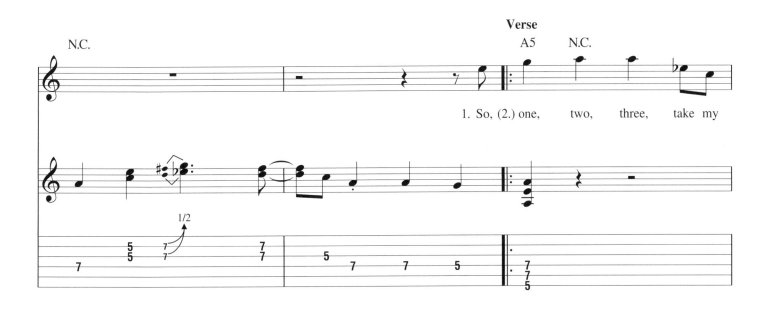

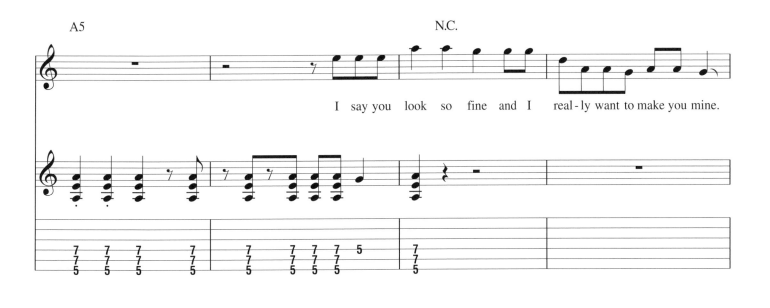

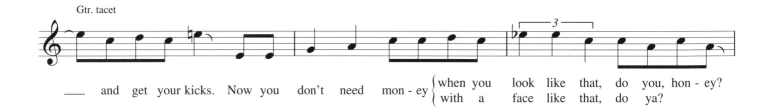

Gtr. tacet

___ and get your kicks. Now you don't need mon - ey $\begin{cases} \text{when you look like that, do you, hon - ey?} \\ \text{with a face like that, do ya?} \end{cases}$

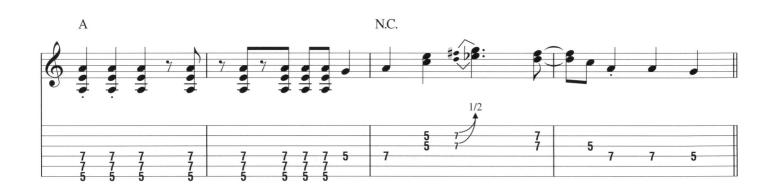

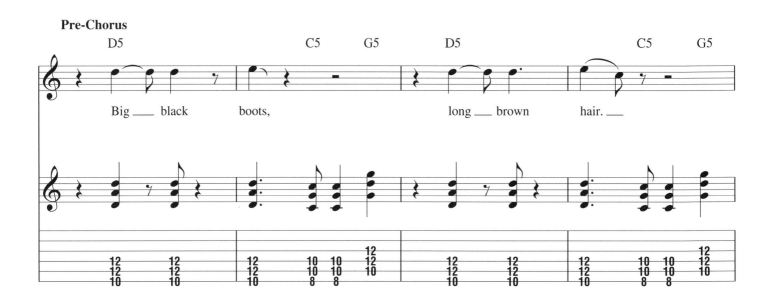

Pre-Chorus

Big ___ black boots, long ___ brown hair. ___

She's ___ so sweet with ___ her get ___ back stare.

Chorus

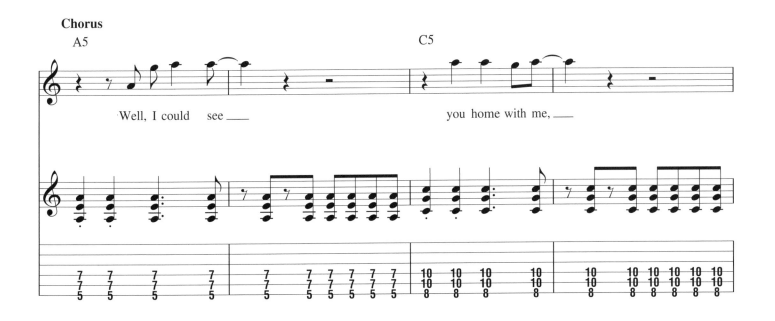

Well, I could see ___ you home with me, ___

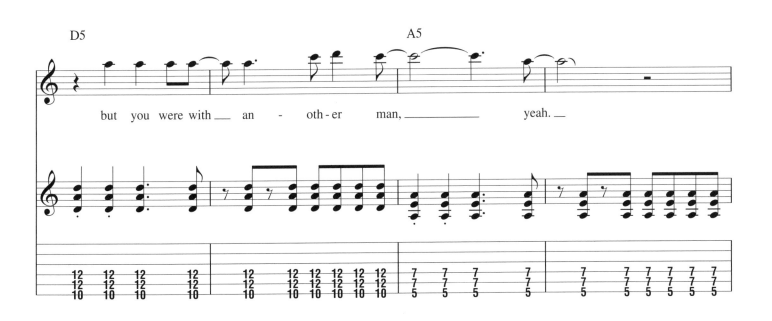

but you were with ___ an-oth-er man, ___ yeah. ___

I ___ know we ain't _ got much to say ___

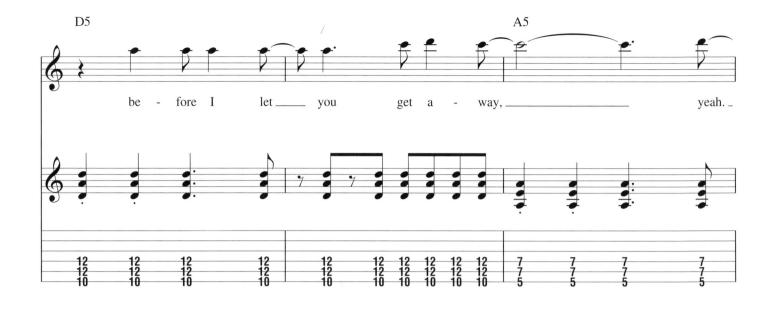

be - fore I let___ you get a - way,_____ yeah. _

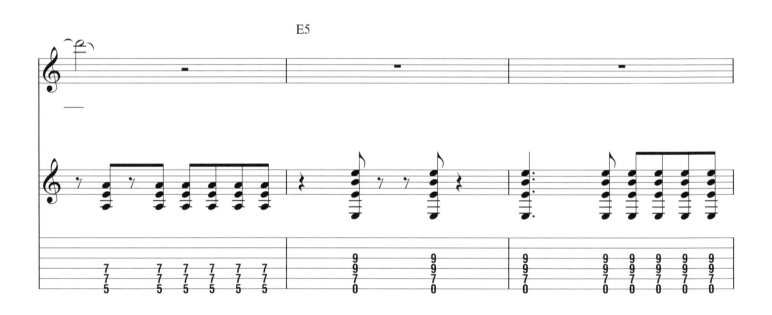

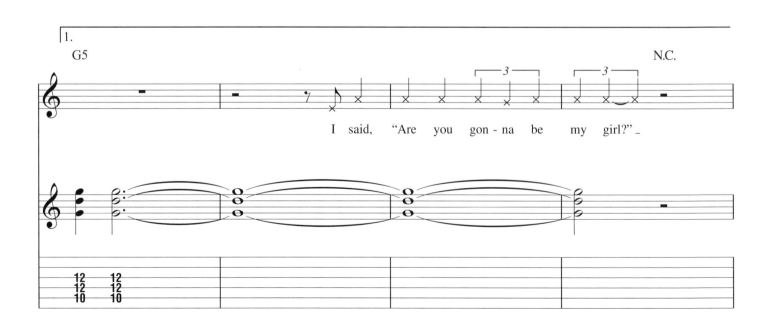

I said, "Are you gon - na be my girl?" _

2. Well, it's a

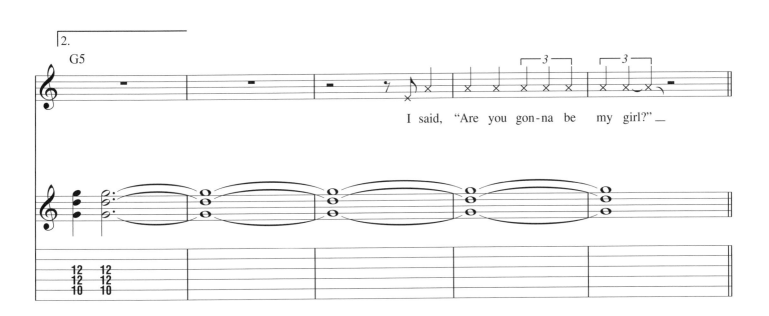

I said, "Are you gon-na be my girl?" —

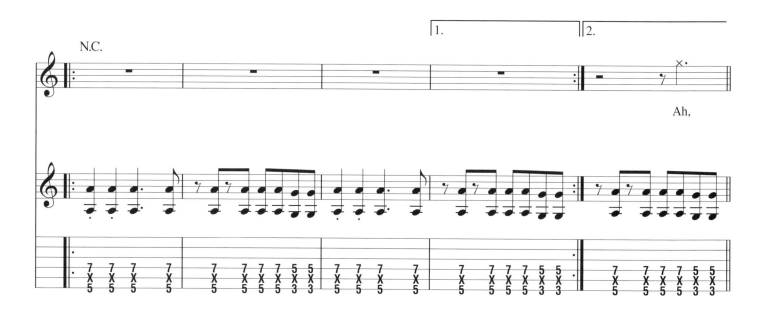

N.C.

1.

2.

Ah,

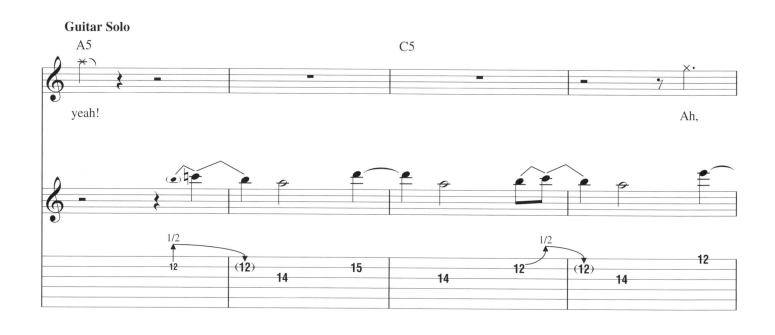

Guitar Solo

A5   C5

yeah!   Ah,

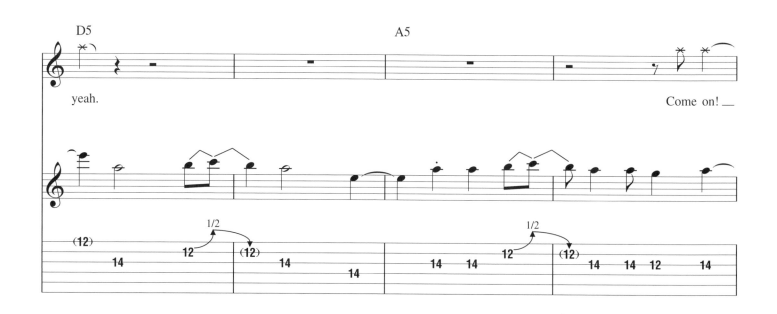

D5   A5

yeah.   Come on! __

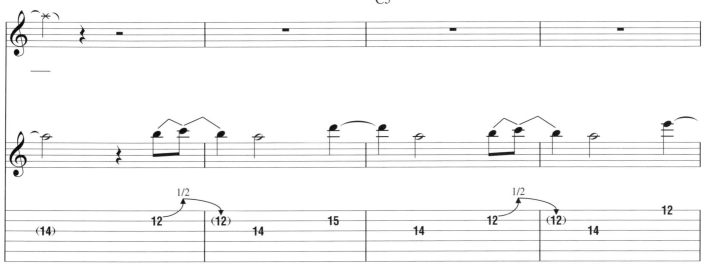

C5

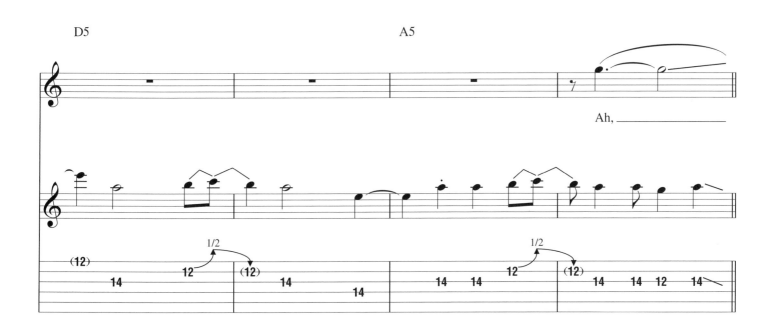

D5   A5

Ah, _____

Chorus

A5   C5

_____ I could see ____   you home with me, ____

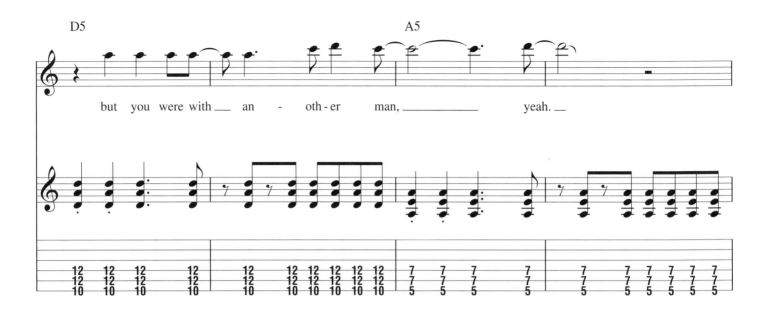

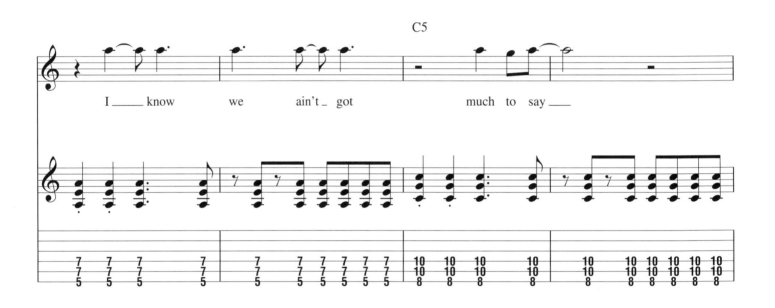

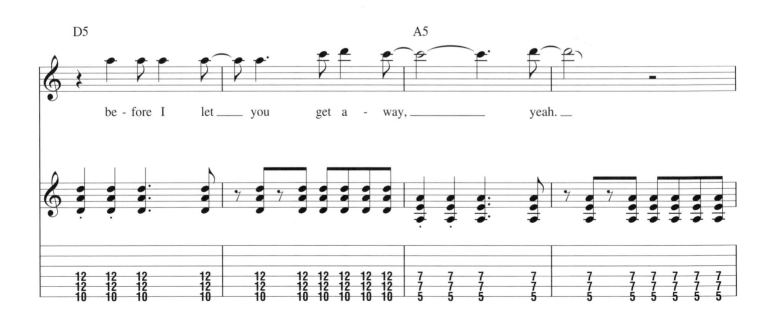

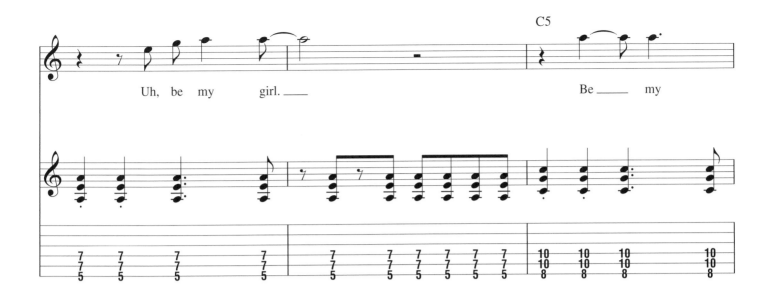

Uh, be my girl. ____   Be ____ my

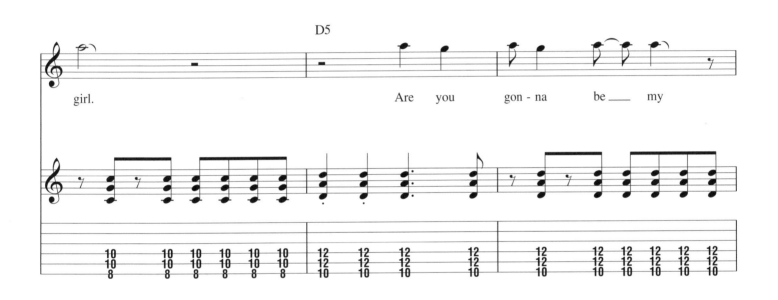

girl.   Are you   gon-na   be ____ my

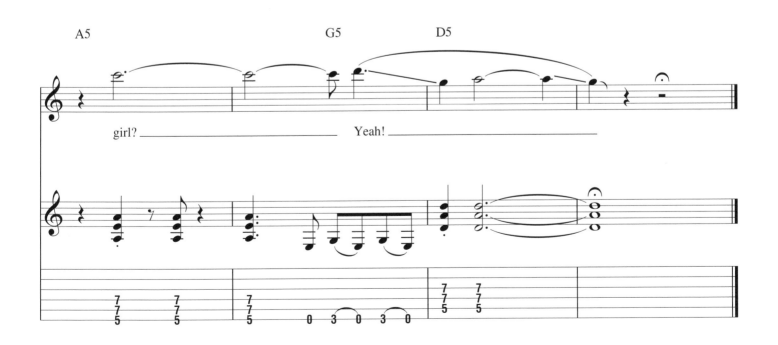

girl? _____   Yeah! _____

Buddy Holly

Words and Music by Rivers Cuomo

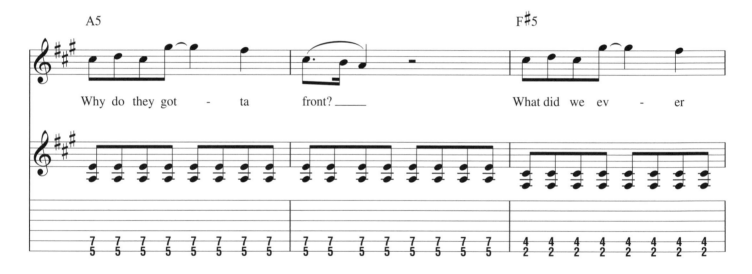

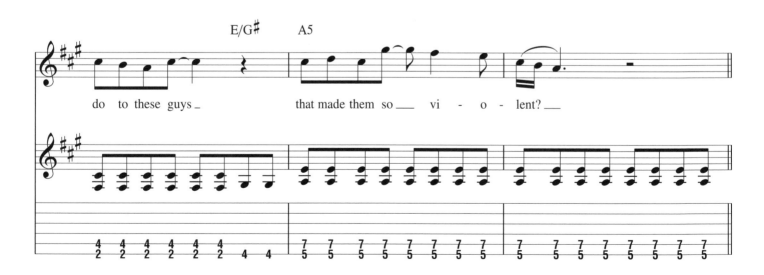

Pre-Chorus

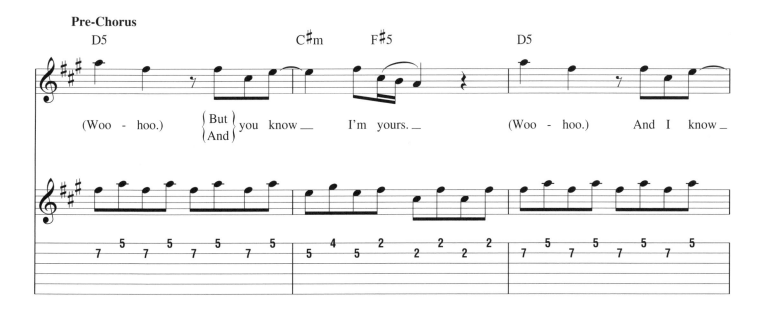

(Woo - hoo.) {But / And} you know __ I'm yours. __ (Woo - hoo.) And I know __

__ you're mine. __ (Woo - hoo. And that's __ for all _____ time.)

Chorus

Woo - ee - oo, I look just like Bud - dy Hol - ly. Oh, oh, and you're

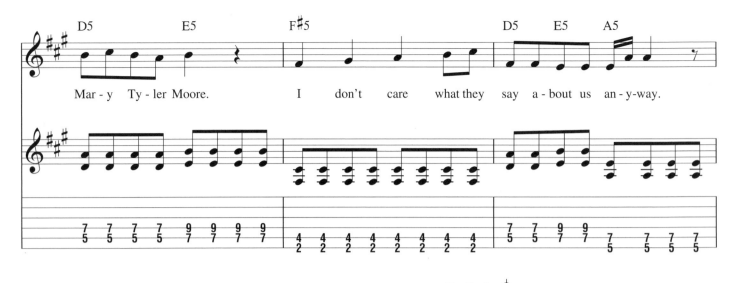

Mar-y Ty-ler Moore. I don't care what they say a-bout us an-y-way.

To Coda ⊕

Interlude

I don't care 'bout that.

D.C. al Coda

⊕ **Coda**

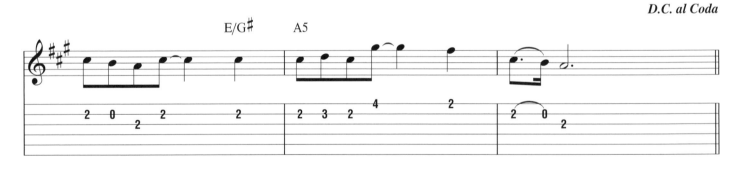

Bridge

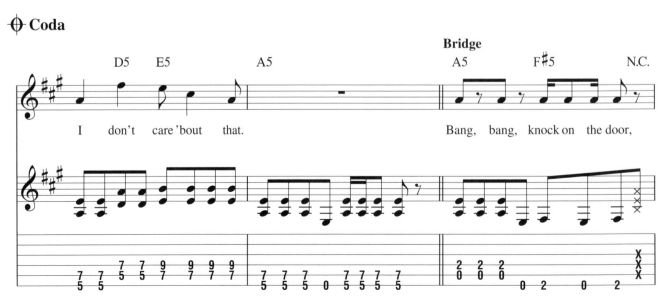

I don't care 'bout that. Bang, bang, knock on the door,

'noth-er big bang, you're down — on the floor. Oh no, what do I do? —

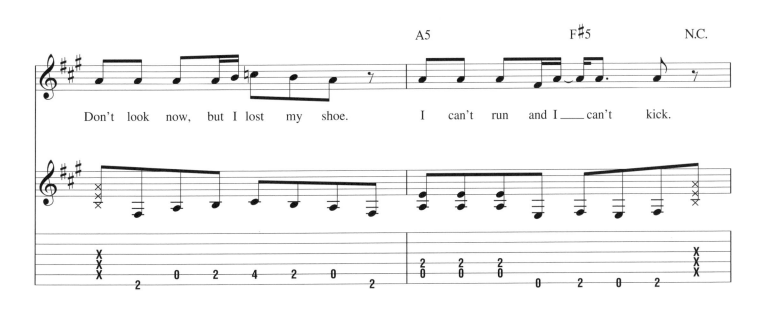

Don't look now, but I lost my shoe. I can't run and I — can't kick.

What's a mat-ter, babe, are you feel - in' sick? What's a mat-ter, what's a mat-ter, what's a mat-ter you?

Guitar Solo

What's a mat-ter, babe, are you feel - in' blue? Oh,   oh,   oh, __ oh,   oh,   oh,   oh,   oh. __

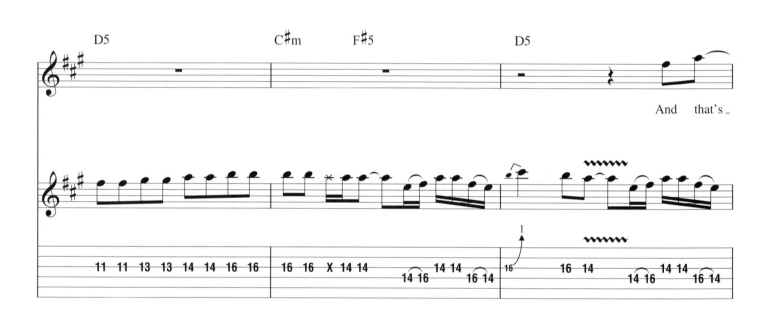

And   that's __

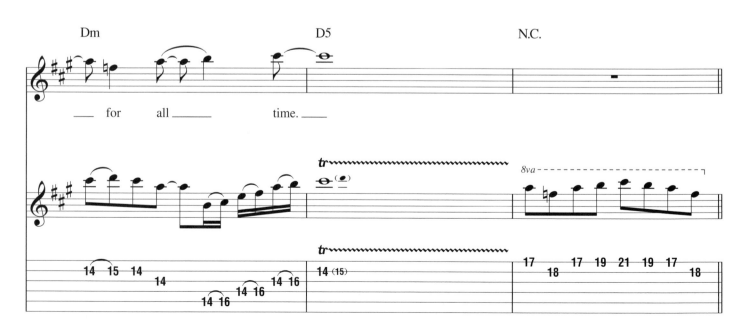

__ for   all _____   time. ____

Outro-Chorus

Woo - ee - oo, I look just like Bud - dy Hol - ly. Oh, oh, and you're

Mar - y Ty - ler Moore. I don't care what they say a - bout us an - y-way.

I don't care 'bout that.

Additional Lyrics

2. Don't you ever fear, I'm always near.
I know that you need help.
Your tongue is twisted, your eyes are slit.
You need a guardian.

Everybody Hurts

Words and Music by William Berry, Peter Buck, Michael Mills and Michael Stipe

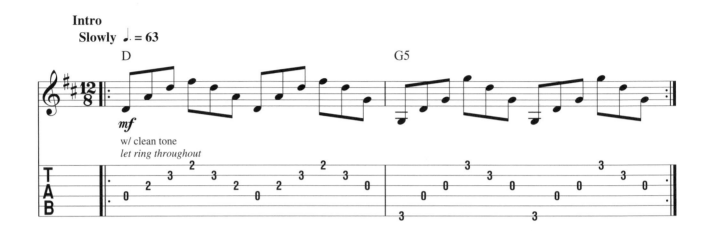

*2nd time, dist. off

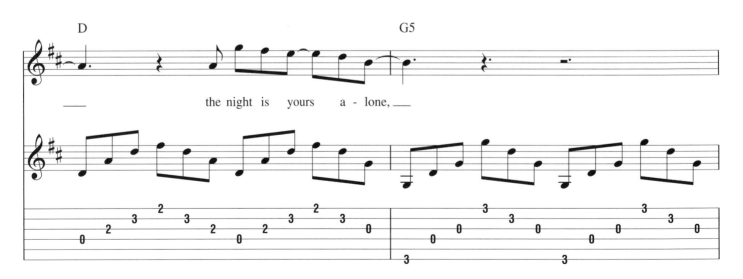

when you're sure   you've___ had e - nough_____   of this life,_

2. *See additional lyrics*

___   well, hang   on. ___

Don't let your - self   go,

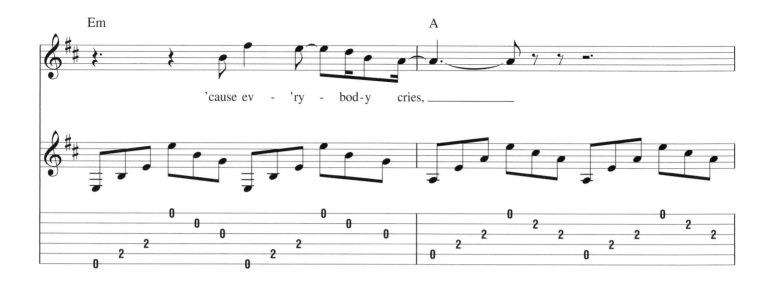

'cause ev - 'ry - bod-y cries, _____

To Coda 1 ✛
To Coda 2 ✛

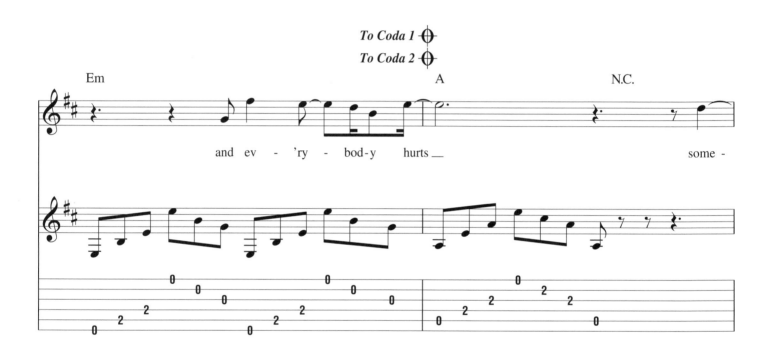

and ev - 'ry - bod-y hurts ___ some -

- times. ___ Some-times ev - 'ry-thing is

wrong. _____

Now it's time __ to sing a-

Verse

2. When your day __ is night __ a - lone,
long. (Hold _____ on. _____ Hold __

D.S. al Coda 1

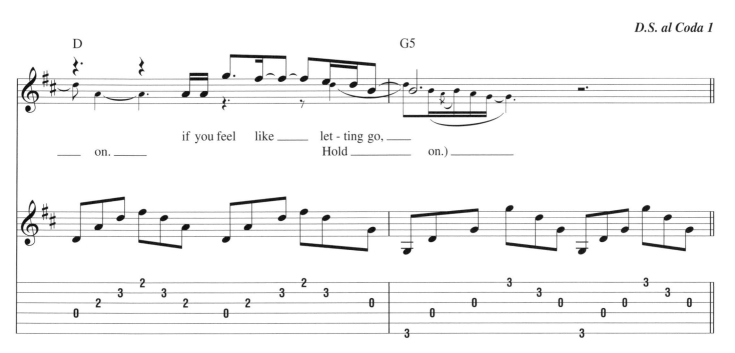

if you feel like _____ let - ting go, _____
__ on. _____ Hold _____ on.) _____

⊕ Coda 1

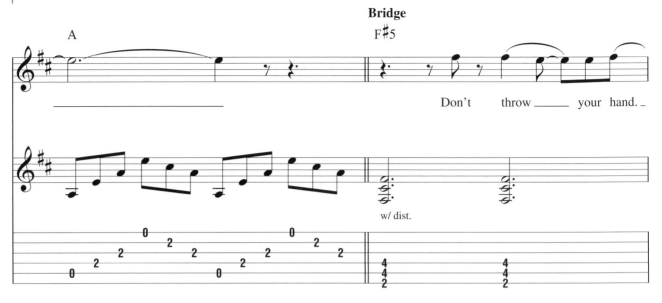

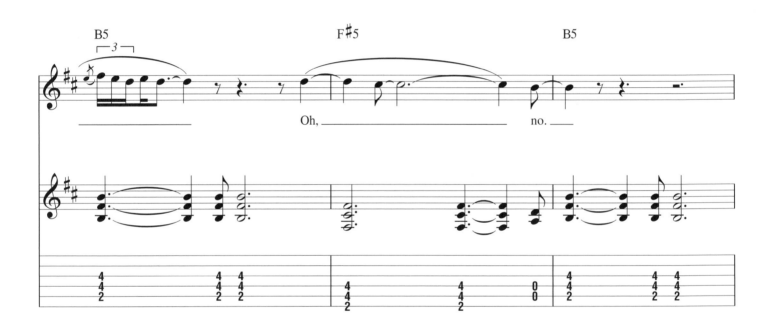

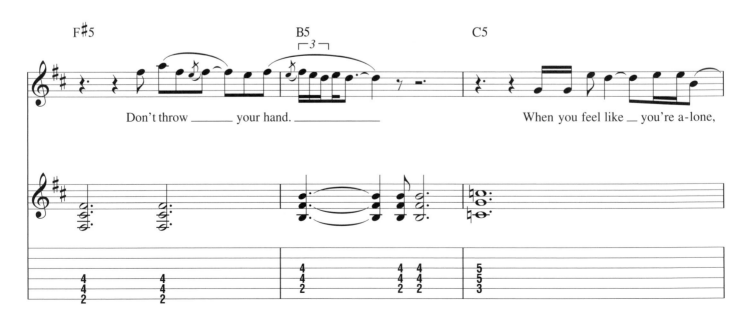

no,   no,   no,   you're not a - lone. ____

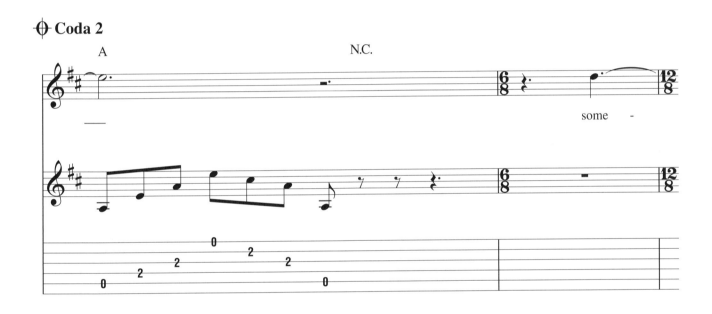

Coda 2

some -

- times. ____   And ev - 'ry - bod-y hurts ____

Outro

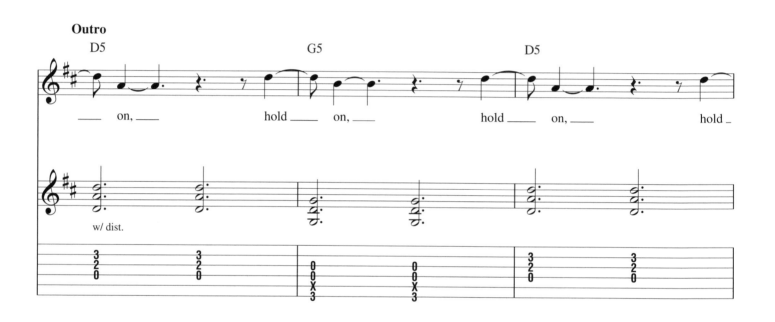

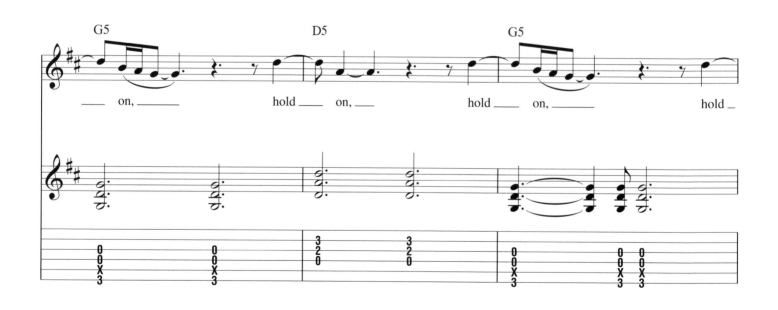

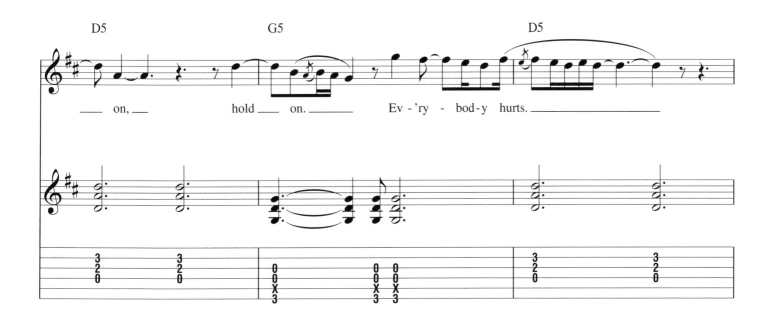

on, ___   hold ___ on. ___   Ev - 'ry - bod-y hurts. ___

Repeat and fade

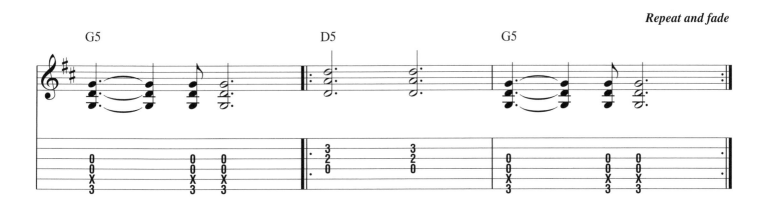

Additional Lyrics

2. When your day is night alone, if you feel like letting go,
   If you think you've had too much of this life, well, hang on.
   'Cause ev'rybody hurts; take comfort in your friends.
   Ev'rybody hurts.

3. If you're on your own in this life, the days and nights are long,
   When you think you've had too much of this life to hang on,
   Well, ev'rybody hurts. Sometimes ev'rybody cries.
   Ev'rybody hurts sometimes. And ev'rybody hurts sometimes.

In Bloom

Words and Music by Kurt Cobain

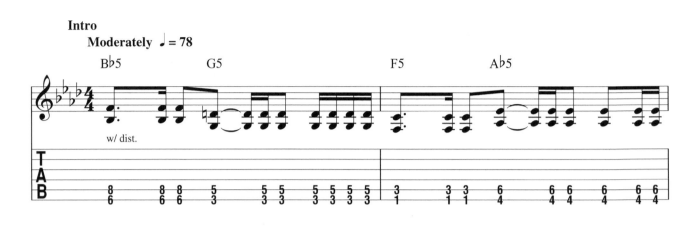

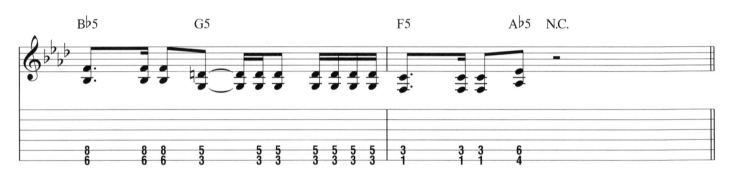

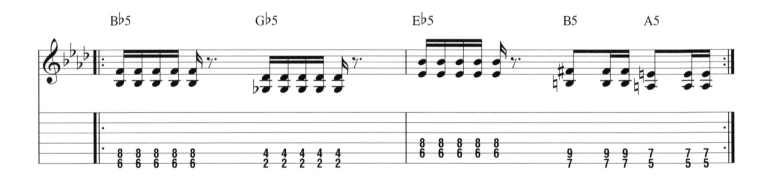

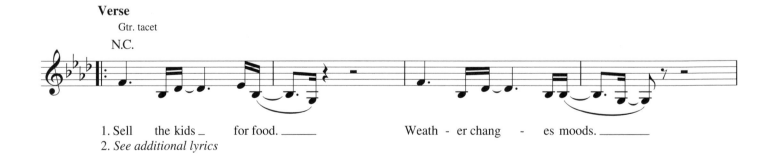

1. Sell the kids _ for food. _____ Weath - er chang - es moods. _____
2. *See additional lyrics*

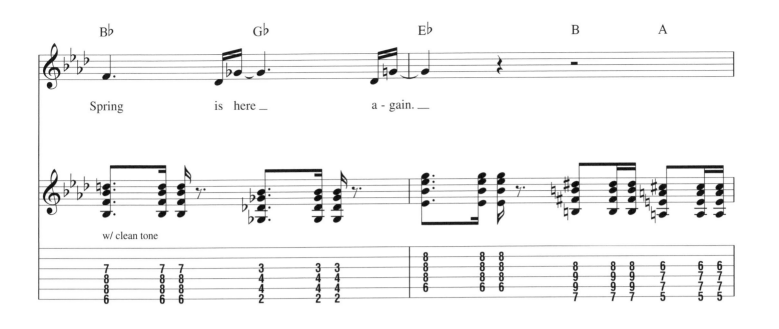

Spring is here _ a - gain. _

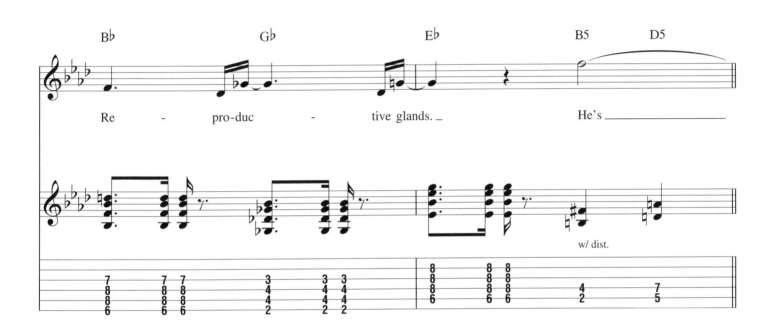

Re - pro-duc - tive glands. _ He's _____

𝄋 Chorus

_ the one _ who likes all our pret-ty songs _ and he

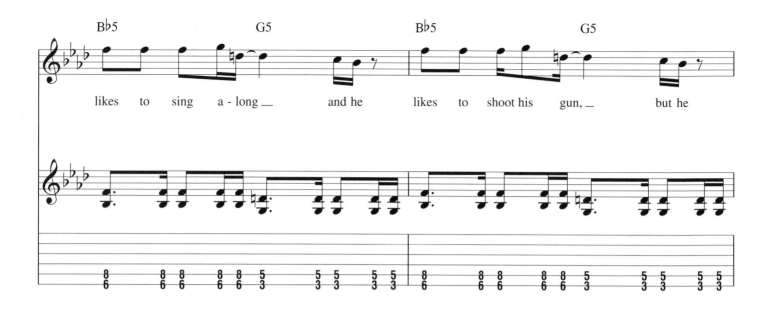

likes to sing a-long __ and he likes to shoot his gun, __ but he

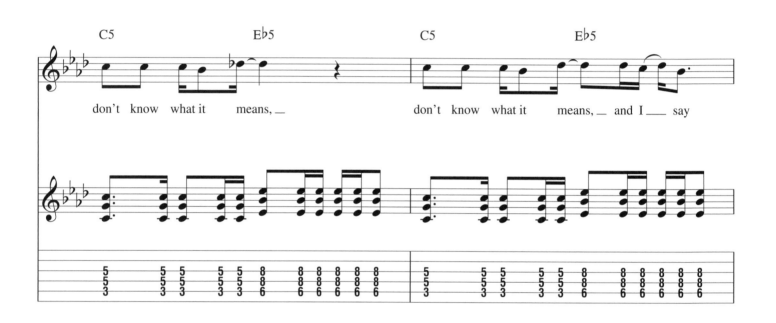

don't know what it means, __ don't know what it means, __ and I __ say

he's the one __ who likes all our pret-ty songs __ and he

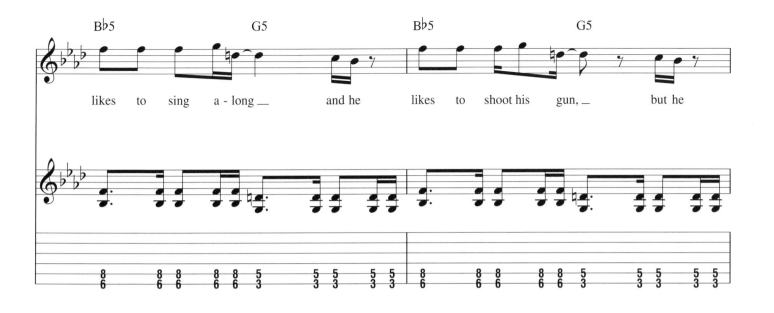

likes   to   sing   a - long ___   and he   likes   to   shoot his   gun, ___   but he

To Coda

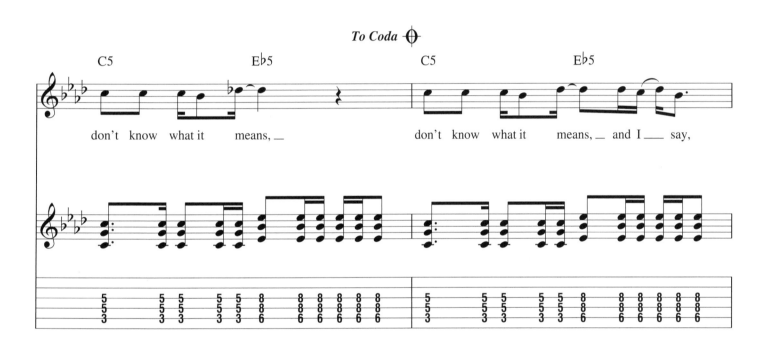

don't   know   what it   means, ___   don't   know   what it   means, ___ and I ___ say,

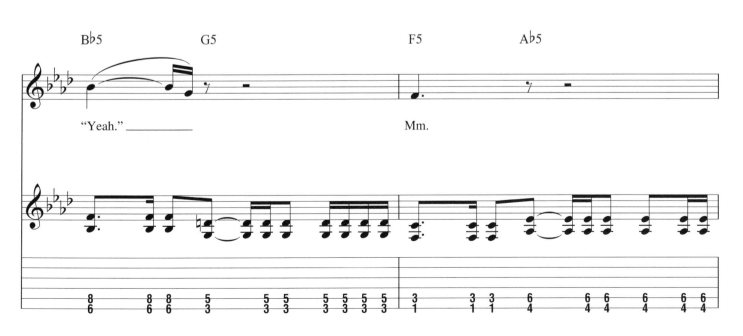

"Yeah." _____   Mm.

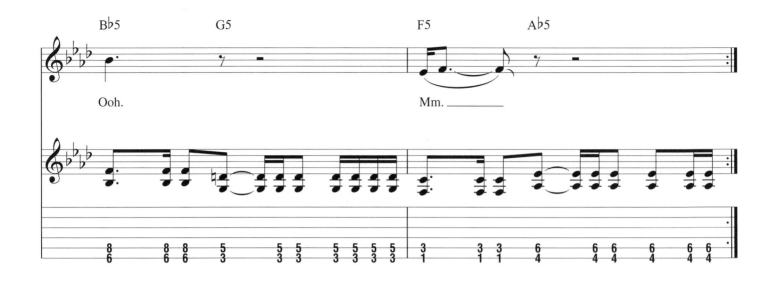

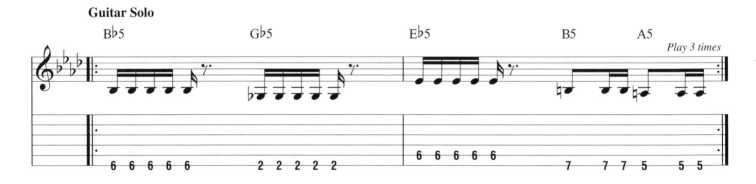

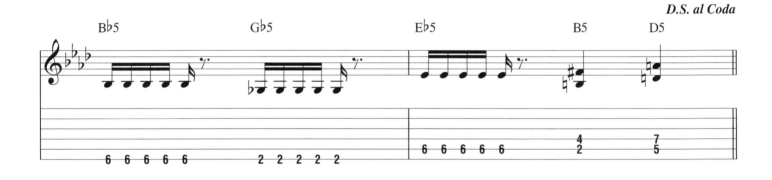

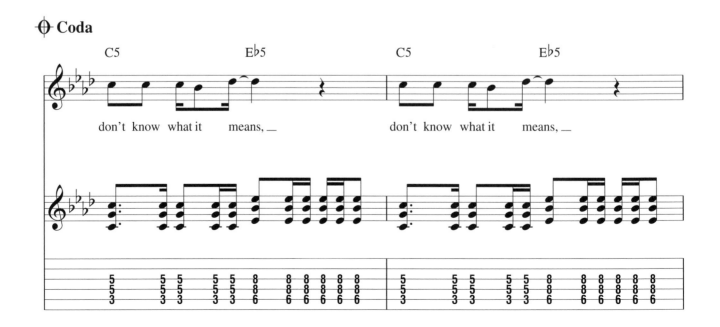

don't know what it means, __ and I __ say,   "Yeah. _____
                                                 Ooh. _____

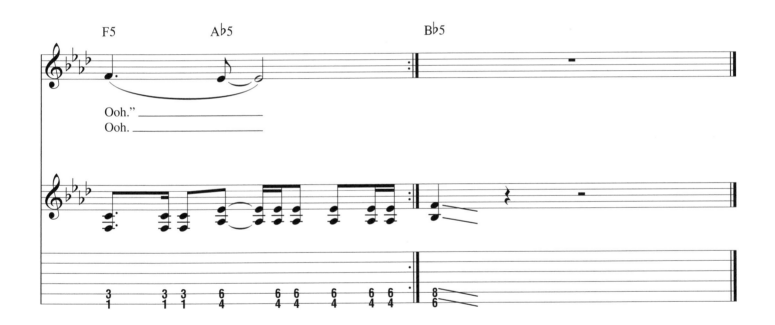

Ooh." _____
Ooh. _____

Additional Lyrics

2. We can have some more.
   Nature is a whore.
   Bruises on the fruit.
   Tender age in bloom.

The Rock Show

Words and Music by Tom De Longe, Mark Hoppus and Travis Barker

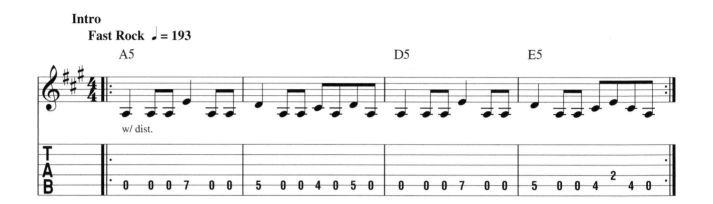

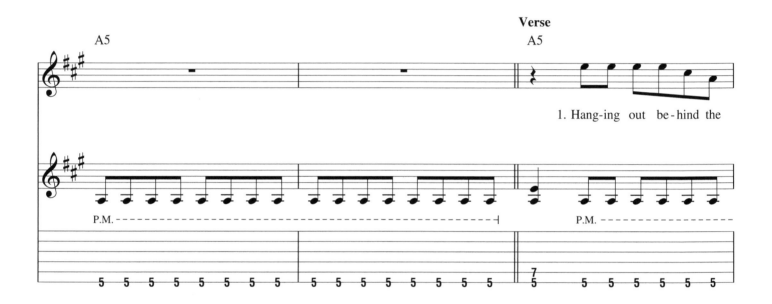

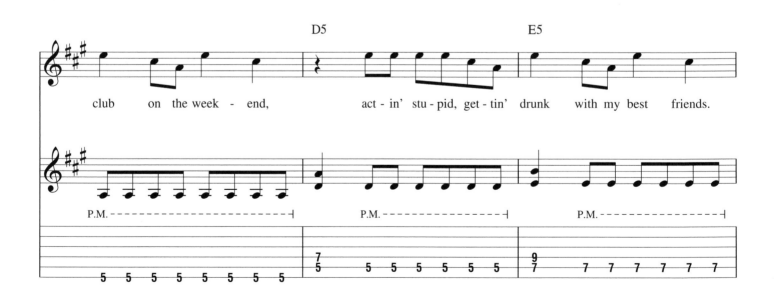

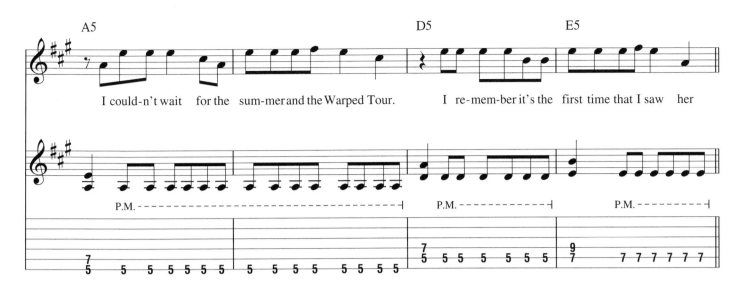

I could-n't wait for the sum-mer and the Warped Tour. I re-mem-ber it's the first time that I saw her

Interlude

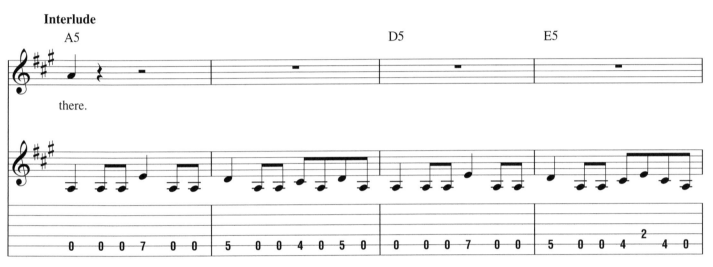

there.

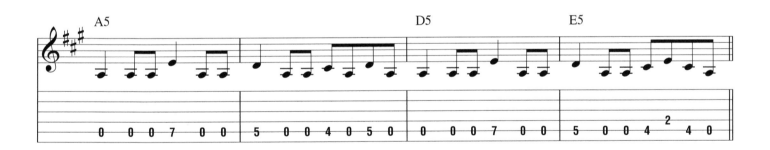

Verse

2. She's get-tin' kicked out of school 'cause she's fail-ing. I'm kind-a ner-vous 'cause I think all her friends hate me.

She's the one, she'll al - ways be there. She took my hand and that made it. I swear be-cause I

𝄋 Chorus

{1., 3. fell / 2. Fell} in love with the girl at the rock show. She said, "What?" And I

told her that I did - n't know. She's so cool. I'm gon - na sneak in through her win - dow.

Ev - 'ry-thing's bet - ter when she's a - round. I can't wait 'til her par - ents go

out of town. I fell in love with the girl at the rock show.

Interlude

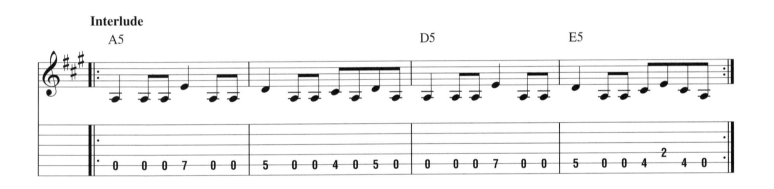

Verse

3. When we said we were gon-na move to Veg - as, I re-mem - ber the look her moth-er gave us.

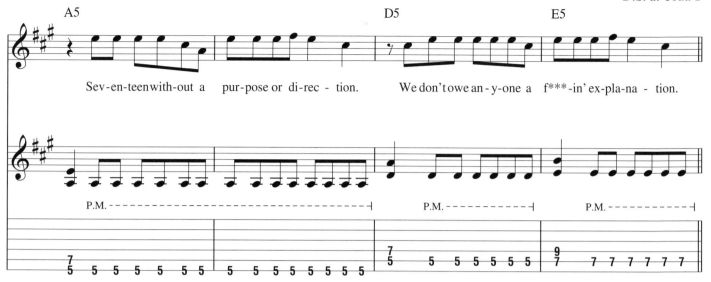

Sev-en-teen with-out a pur-pose or di-rec - tion. We don't owe an-y-one a f***-in' ex-pla-na - tion.

Coda 1

Bridge

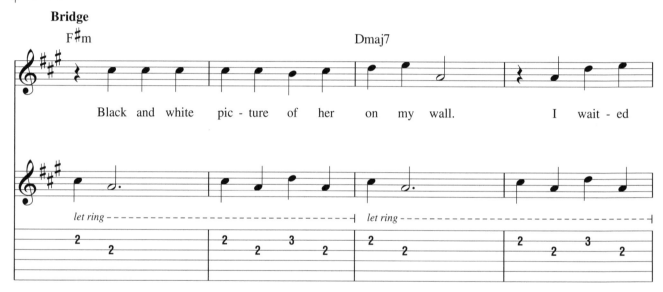

Black and white pic - ture of her on my wall. I wait - ed

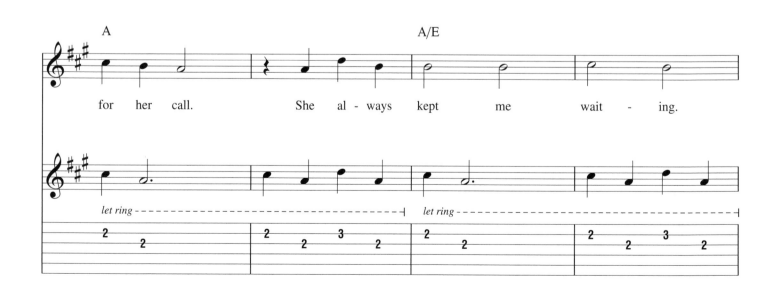

for her call. She al - ways kept me wait - ing.

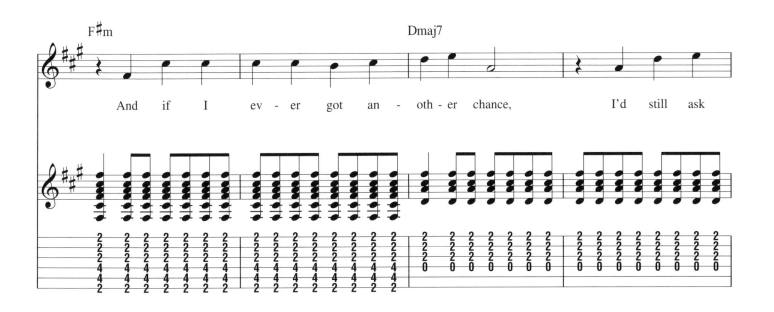

And if I ev-er got an-oth-er chance, I'd still ask

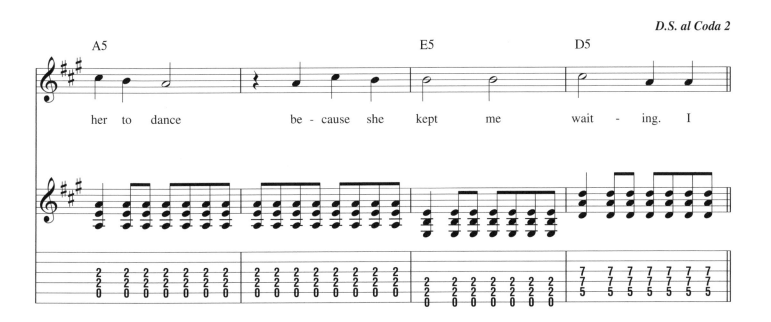

D.S. al Coda 2

her to dance be-cause she kept me wait-ing. I

Coda 2

Repeat and fade

Outro

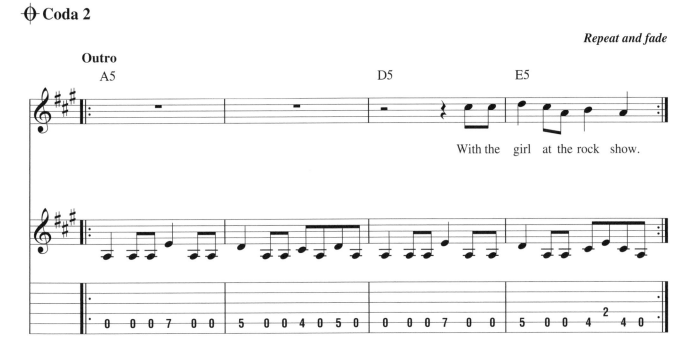

With the girl at the rock show.

Otherside

Words and Music by Anthony Kiedis, Flea, John Frusciante and Chad Smith

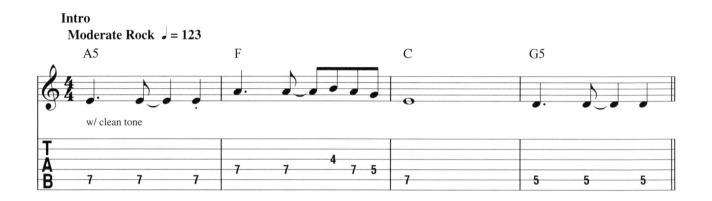

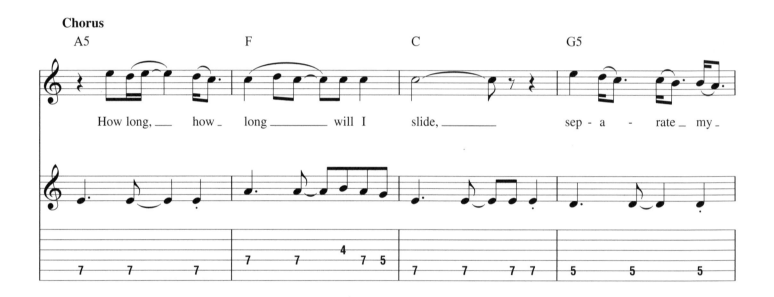

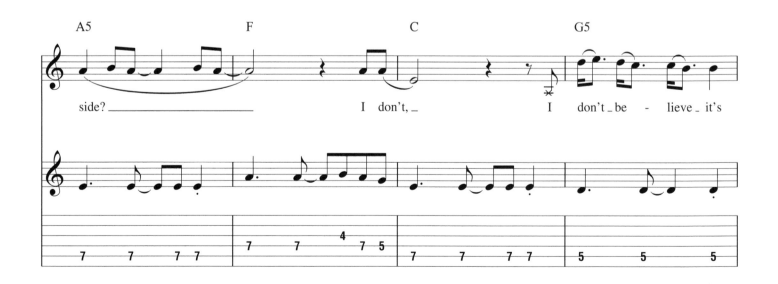

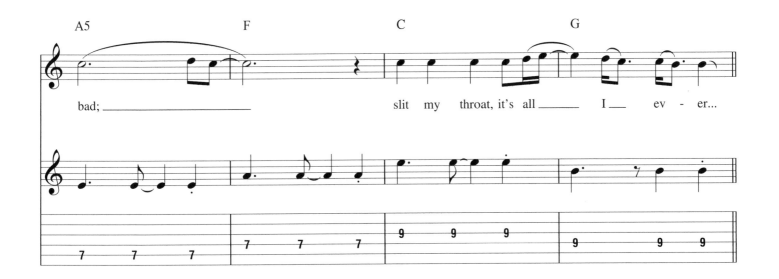

bad; _____ slit my throat, it's all _____ I ___ ev - er...

Verse

1. I heard your voice through a pho - to - graph; ___ I thought it up it brought

up the ___ past. ___ Once you know you can nev - er go back. ___ I've got to

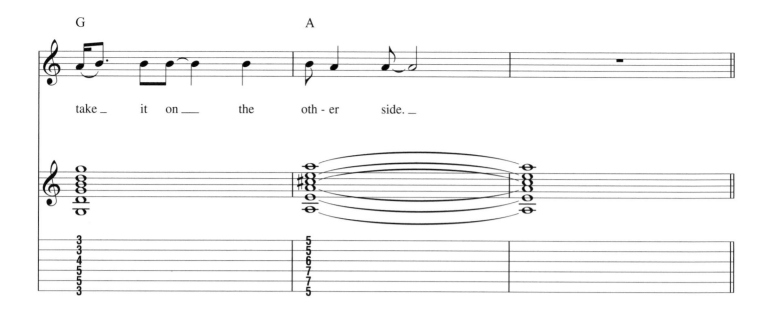

§ Verse

2. Cen - tu - ries are what it meant _ to me; _ a cem - e - ter - y where I
4. *See additional lyrics*

let ring

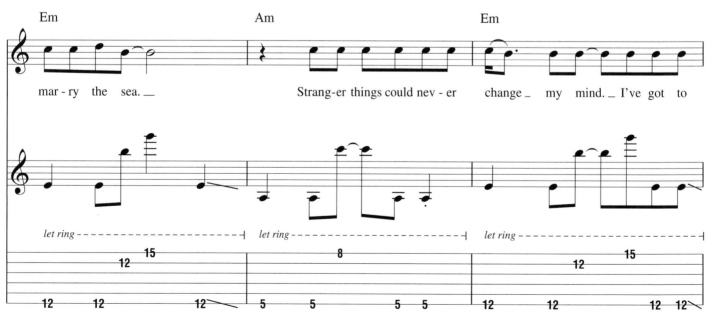

mar - ry the sea. _ Strang - er things could nev - er change _ my mind. _ I've got to

let ring

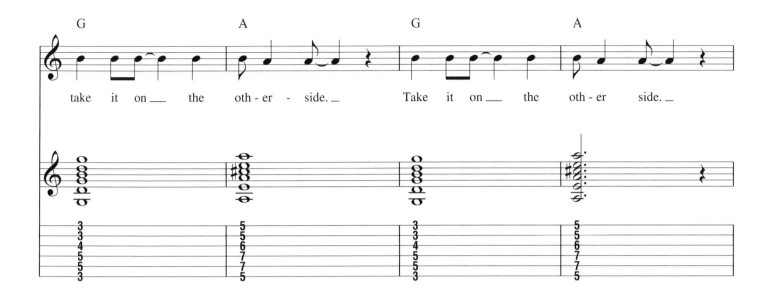

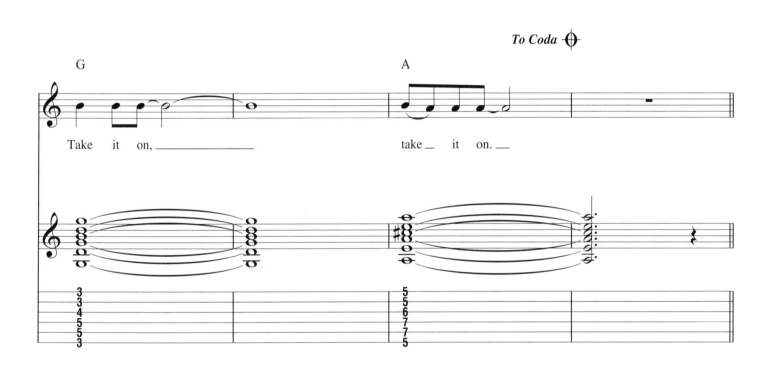

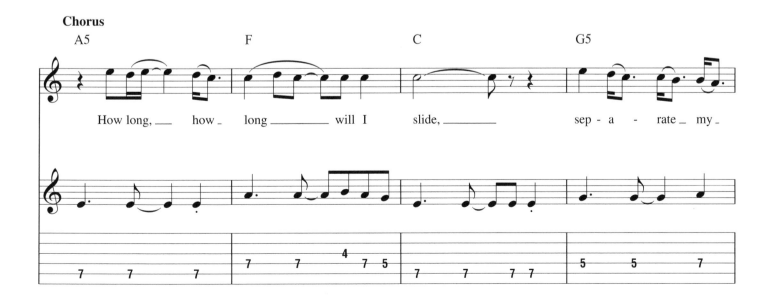

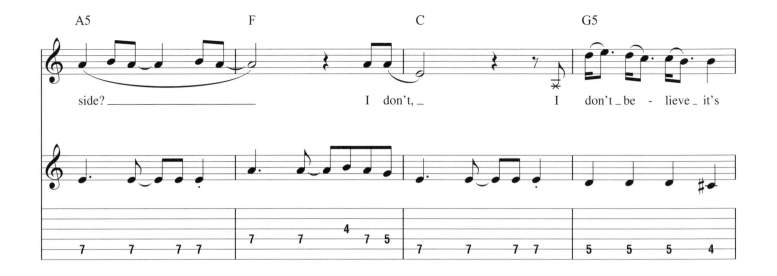

side? _____ I don't, __ I don't _ be - lieve _ it's

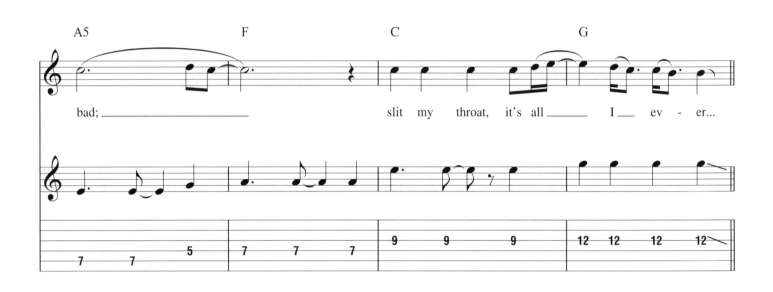

bad; _____ slit my throat, it's all _____ I __ ev - er...

Verse

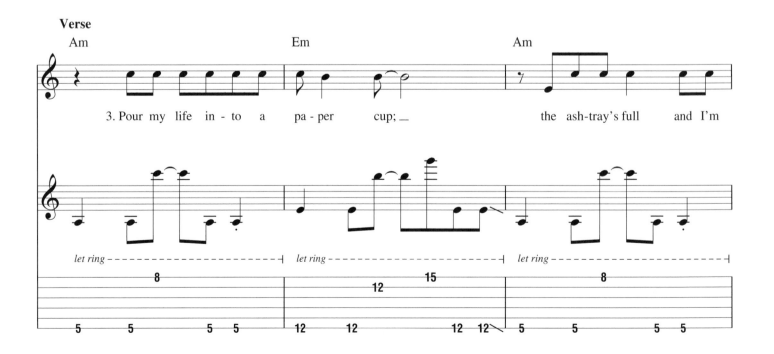

3. Pour my life in - to a pa - per cup; __ the ash-tray's full and I'm

spil - lin' my guts. ___ She wants to know am I still a slut. ___ I've got to

let ring

D.S. al Coda

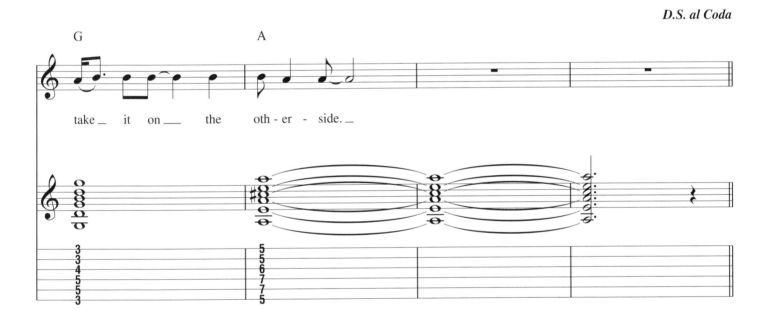

take ___ it on ___ the oth - er - side. ___

Coda

Chorus

How long, ___ how ___ long ___ will I

slide,   sep - a - rate _ my _ side? _____

_   I   don't, _   I   don't _ be - lieve _ it's

bad; _____   a   slit-tin' my   throat,   it's all _____ I _ ev - er.... _

Bridge

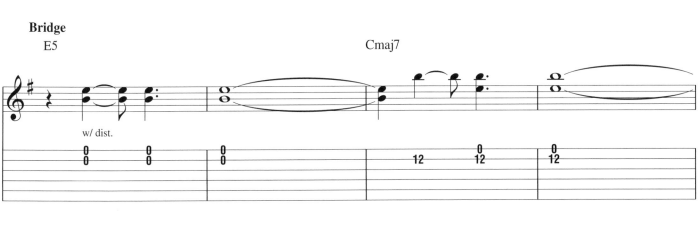

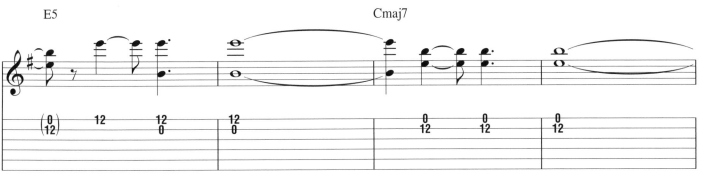

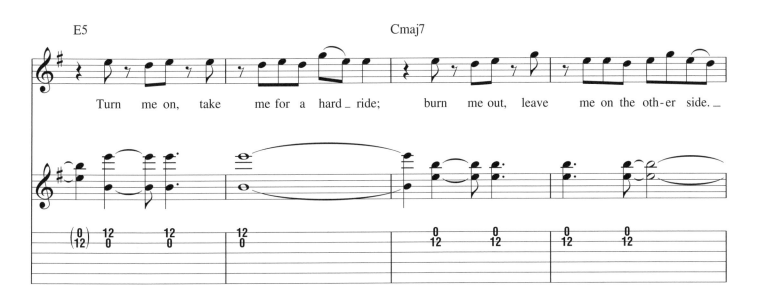

Turn me on, take me for a hard ride; burn me out, leave me on the oth-er side.

I yell and tell it that it's not my friend, I tear it down, I tear it down and then it's born a - gain.

Guitar Solo

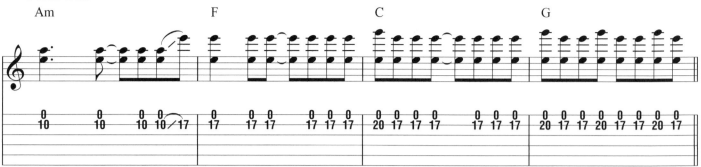

Outro-Chorus

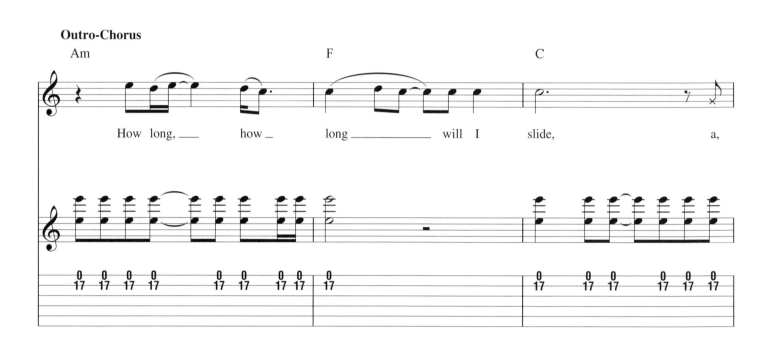

How long, ___ how ___ long _____ will I slide, a,

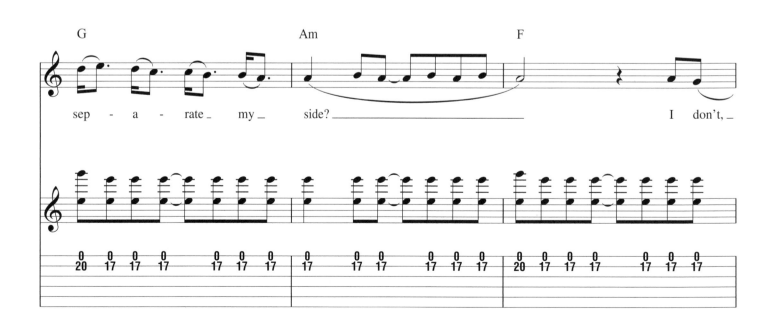

sep - a - rate ___ my ___ side? _____ I don't, ___

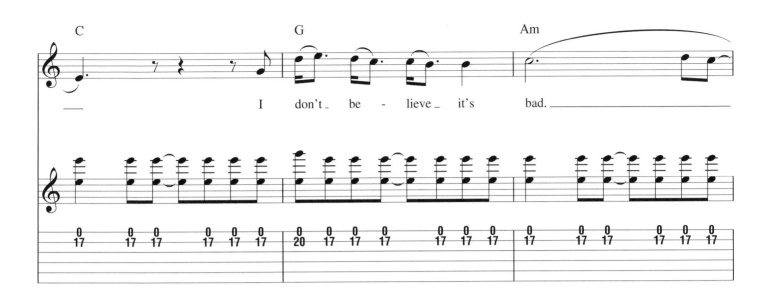

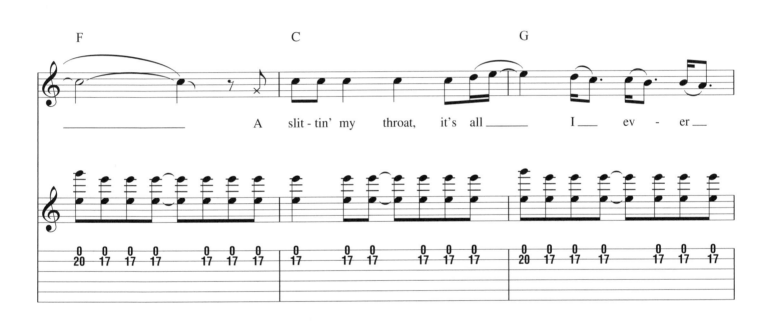

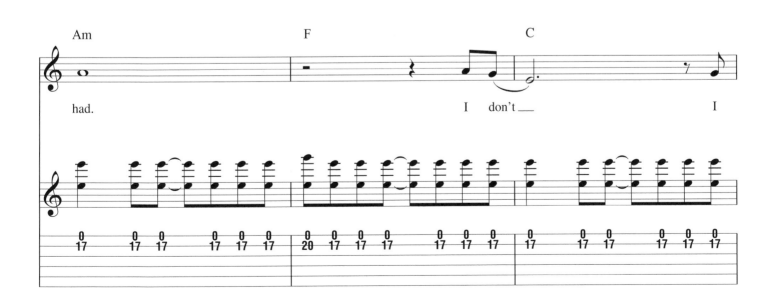

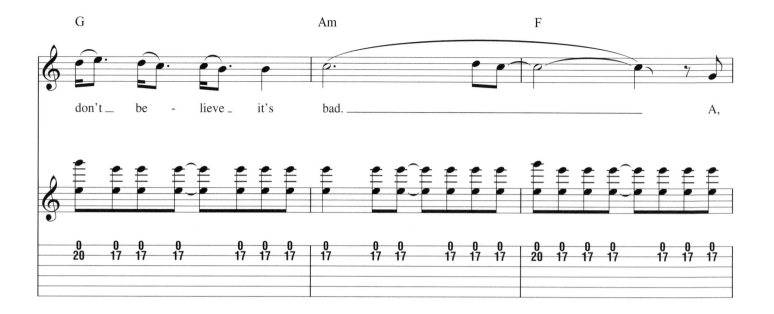

don't __ be - lieve __ it's bad. _____ A,

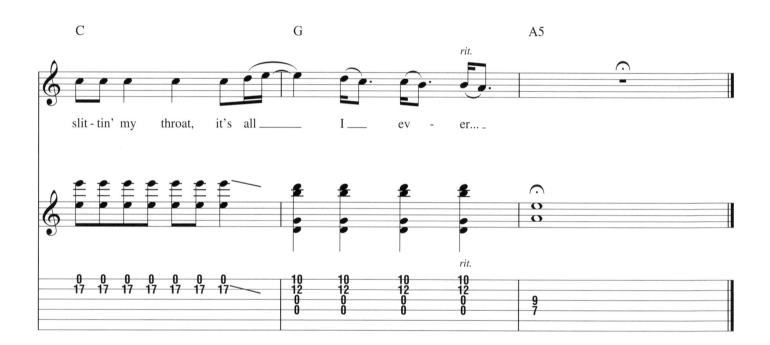

slit - tin' my throat, it's all _____ I __ ev - er... _

Additional Lyrics

4. Scarlet starlet and she's in my bed,
A candidate, a, for my soulmate bled.
Push the trigger and pull the thread.
I've got to take it on the otherside.
Take it on the other side.
Take it on, take it on.

Santa Monica

Words by Art Alexakis
Music by Art Alexakis and Everclear

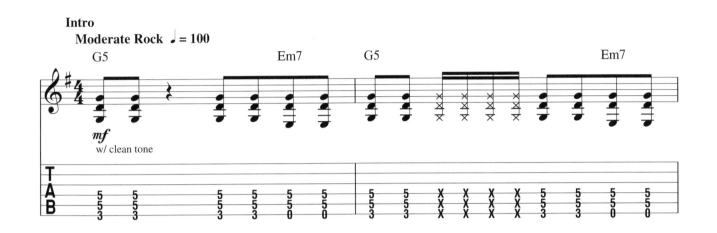

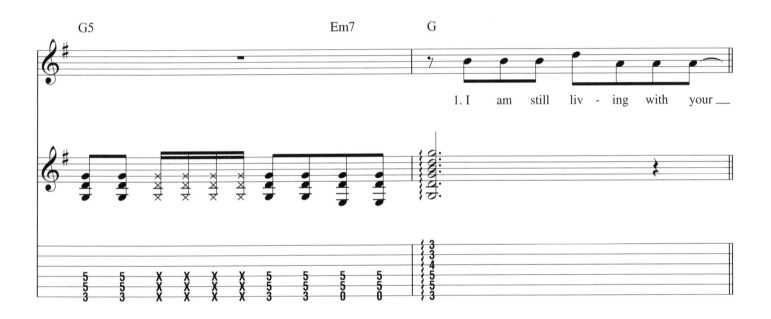

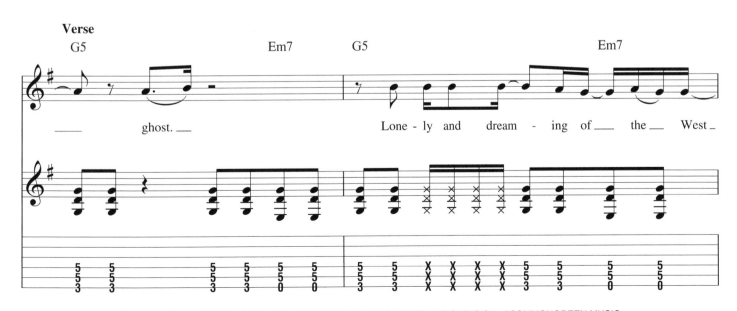

Chorus

this dis-ease. ___ We can live __ be-side __ the o-

-cean, leave the fire __ be-hind. ___ Swim out past __ the break-

-ers, watch the world __ die. ___ We can live __ be-side __ the o-

When I Come Around

Words by Billie Joe
Music by Green Day

Intro
Moderately ♩ = 100

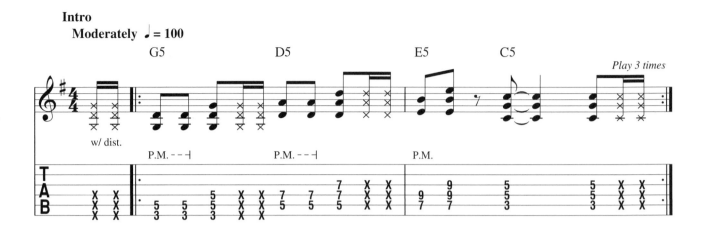

Verse

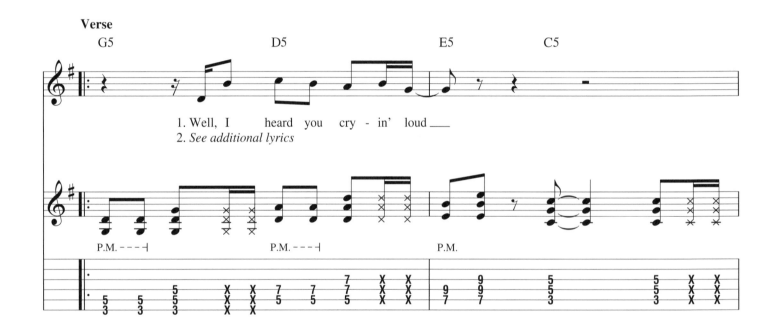

1. Well, I   heard you   cry - in' loud ___
2. *See additional lyrics*

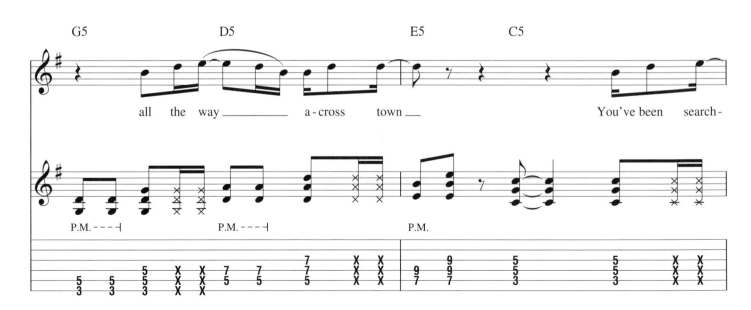

all   the   way ___   a - cross   town ___   You've been   search-

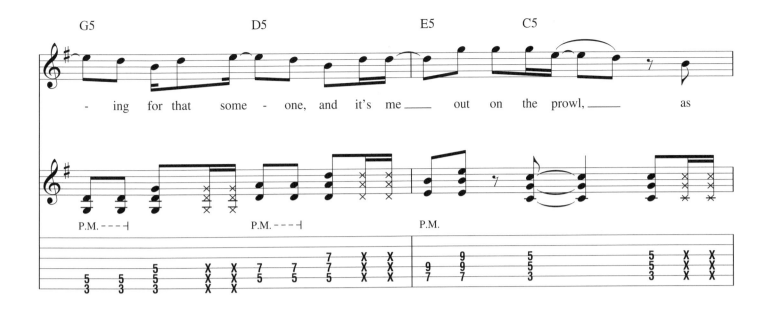

-ing for that some-one, and it's me ___ out on the prowl, ___ as

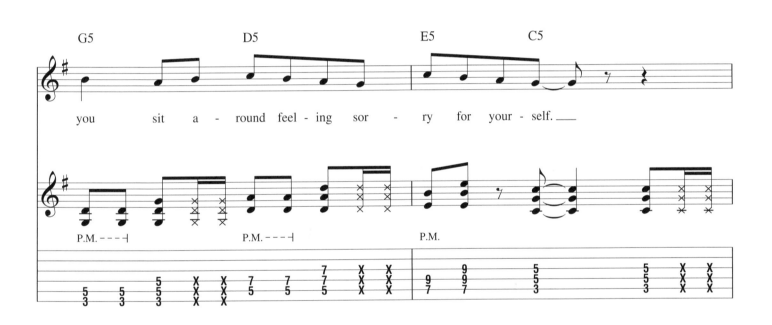

you sit a-round feel-ing sor-ry for your-self. ___

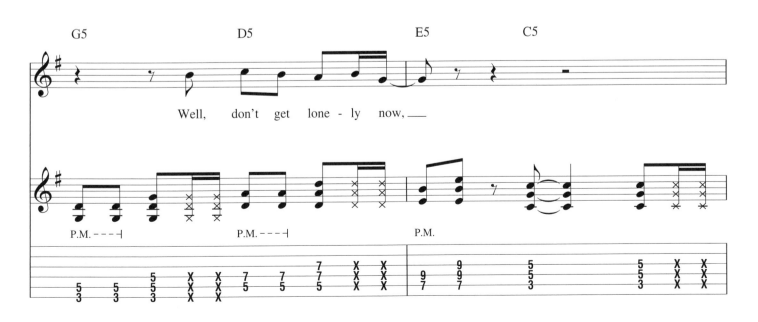

Well, don't get lone-ly now, ___

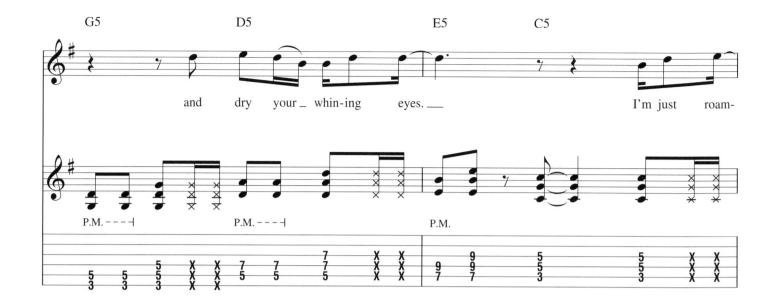

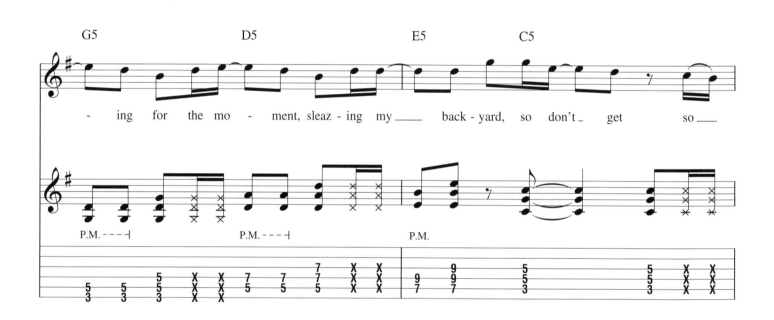

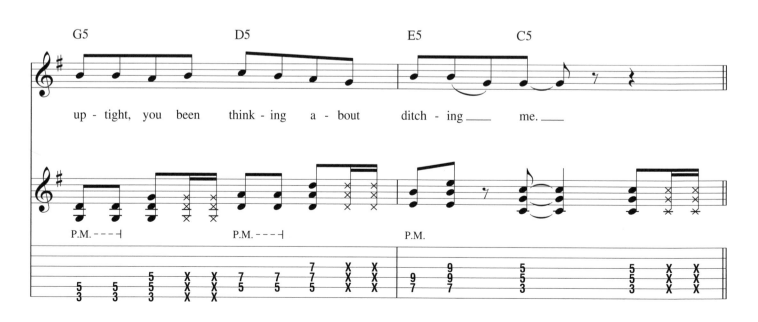

Chorus

No time to search the world a - round,

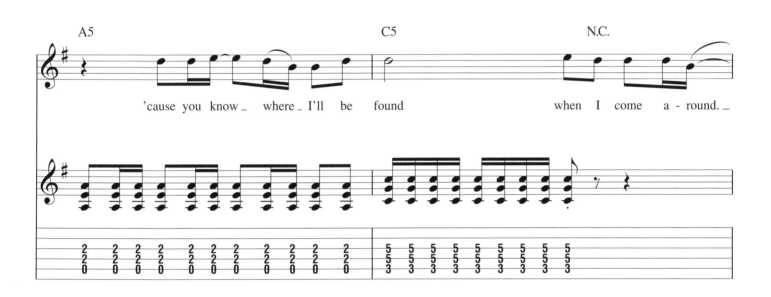

'cause you know ___ where ___ I'll be found when I come a - round. ___

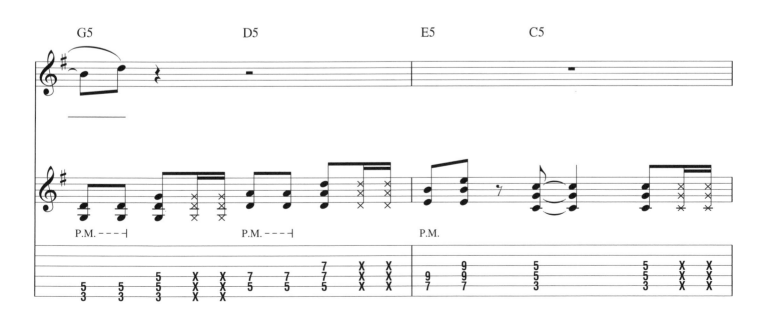

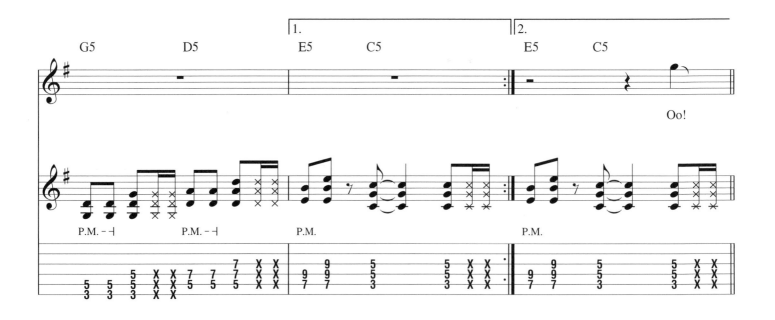

G5   D5 |1.   E5   C5 |2.   E5   C5

Oo!

Guitar Solo

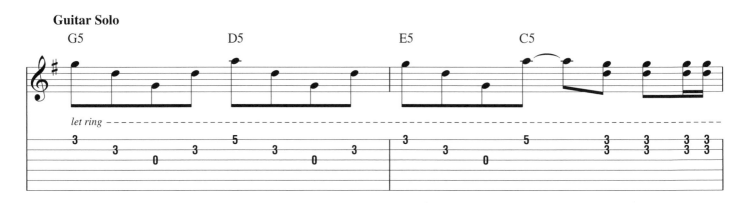

G5   D5   E5   C5

let ring

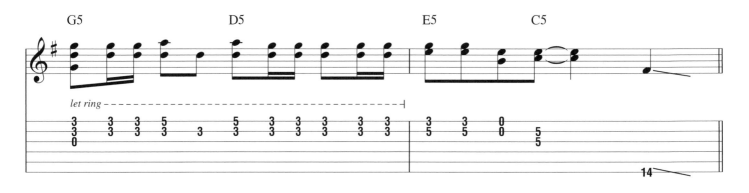

G5   D5   E5   C5

let ring

Chorus

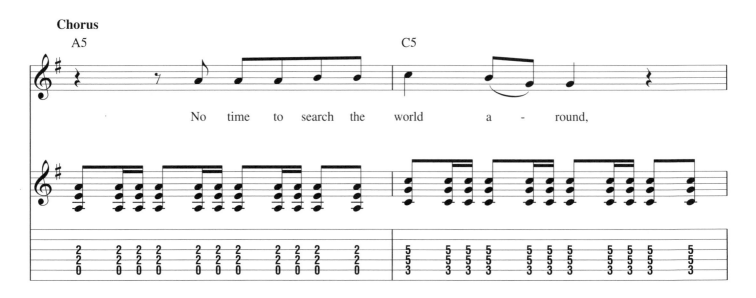

A5   C5

No time to search the world a - round,

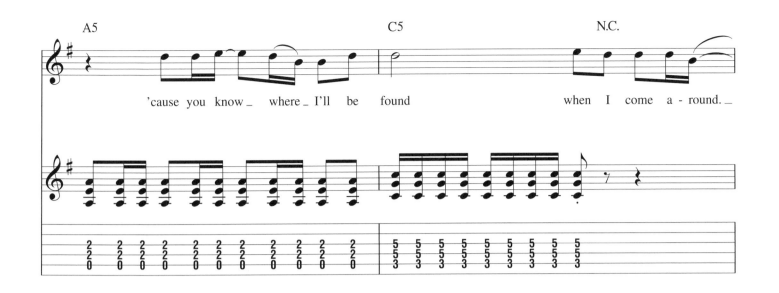

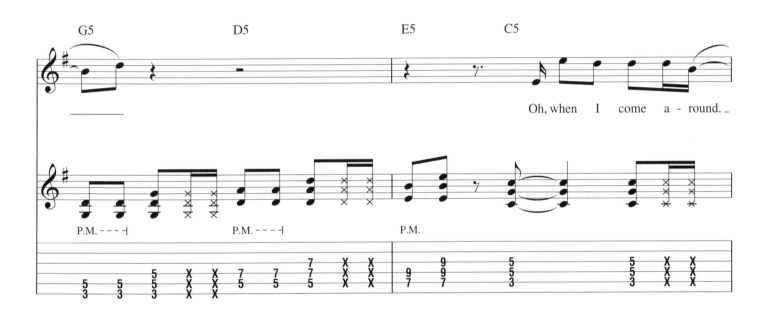

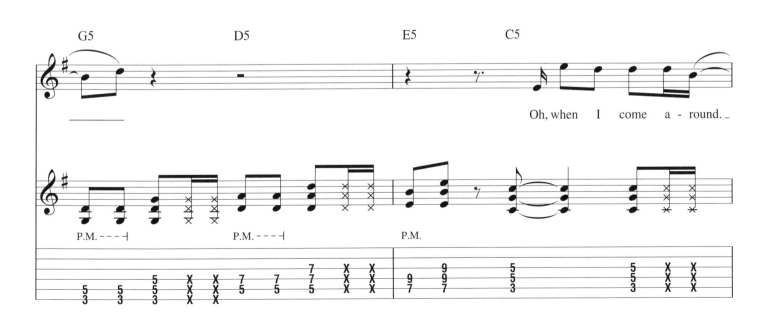

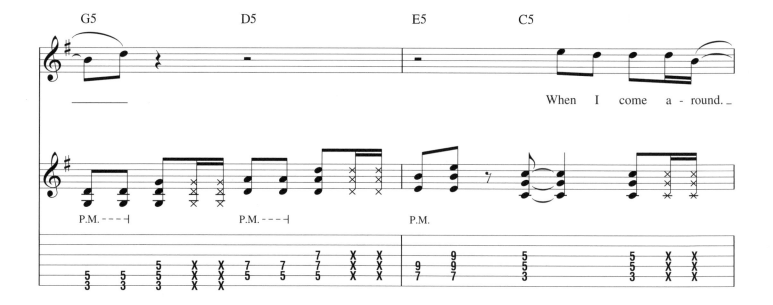

When I come a‑round.

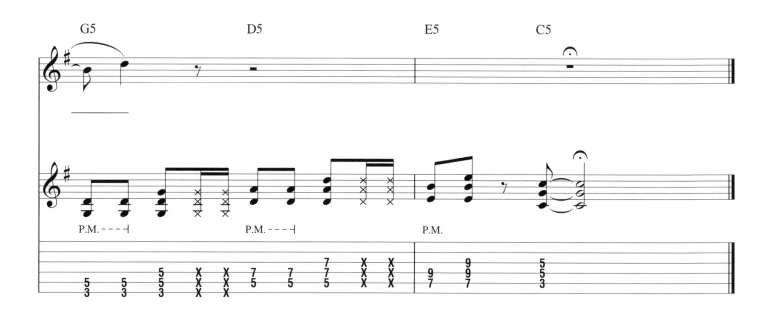

Additional Lyrics

2. Well, I heard it all before, so don't knock down my door.
I'm a loser and a user so I don't need no accuser
To try and slag me down, because I know you're right.
So go do what you like. Make sure you do it wise.
You might find out that your self-doubt means nothing was ever there.
You can't go forcing something if it's just not right.